MW00948538

Milo Loves the Park

Written by: Nancy G. Braitman

Illustrated by S.Buonanno

Come to the park with Milo and me,
To see pretty flowers, birds and bees

Over the hills and near the trees,
it's so fun to walk in the soft breeze!

In the pond, mom and baby ducks swim,
Milo's excited and jumps right in!

Frisbees soar and fly through the air.

**LOOK! Over there,
it's a fox's lair!**

Dogs bark loud
and are very frisky,

Milo jumps and catches a frisbee!

Gorgeous butterflies flutter and tap,

Milo watches as they dine on sap!

Deer saunter shyly along the path,

walking to the pond to take a bath.

Some days the park is quiet and calm, great for walking with Milo and mom!

Summer is grand and so much fun,
beautiful weather and lots of sun!

Yellow leaves, orange leaves, red ones too!

**Kids piling leaves-look!
The pile grew!**

Winter wonderland with
snow-capped trees,

Milo prances in the snow with ease.

Pink and purple
flowers in the spring!

What else on earth will nature bring?

I like to walk with Milo, Mom and Dad,
Milo chases squirrels and runs like mad!

Milo stares at the beautiful sky,
getting lit up by a firefly.

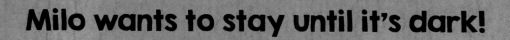

Milo wants to stay until it's dark!

Made in the USA
Middletown, DE
06 April 2024

52561538R00020